CELEBRATING THE FAMILY NAME OF VAZQUEZ

Celebrating the Family Name of Vazquez

Walter the Educator

Silent King Books
a WhichHead Entertainment Imprint

Disclaimer

Celebrating the Family Name of Vazquez is a memory book that belongs to the Celebrating Family Name Book Series by Walter the Educator. Collect them all and more books at WaltertheEducator.com

USE THE EXTRA SPACE TO DOCUMENT YOUR FAMILY MEMORIES THROUGHOUT THE YEARS

The name of Vazquez stands with pride.

Through generations, strong and true,

They face the world with courage new.

The Vazquez heart is bold and bright,

Guided by wisdom, strength, and light.

In storms or peace, they hold their ground,

A steadfast clan, in kinship bound.

Each step they take, each path they tread,

They honor those who came and led.

From ancient lands to new domains,

The Vazquez spirit never wanes.

With hands that labor, minds that soar,

They shape their lives and so much more.

Crafting futures, fierce and free,

The Vazquez name a legacy.

In laughter shared, in sorrow known,

Their strength as one has only grown.

Through trials faced and joys embraced,

Their bonds of love cannot be erased.

Brave and true, with honor worn,

A family proud, a legend born.

Through quiet grace or mighty roar,

The Vazquez name will live once more.

With wisdom earned through time and tears,

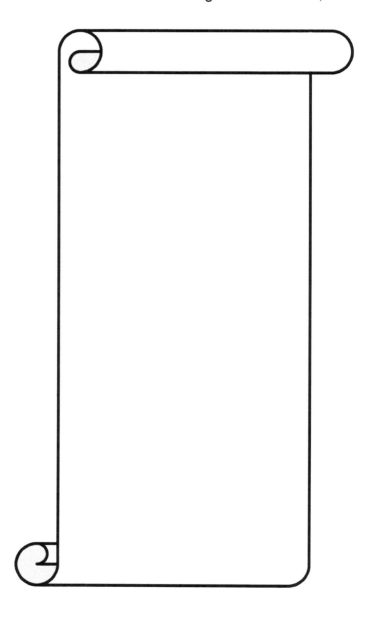

They rise above their doubts and fears.

A clan of heart, of grit and grace,

The Vazquez name knows no disgrace.

Through endless dreams, they reach for more,

With hope and faith in rich rapport.

For in their veins, a fire burns bright,

A torch that guides them through the night.

So raise a glass to all who bear

This treasured name beyond compare.

For Vazquez lives in heart and hand,

A legacy that's truly grand.

With love and strength in all they do,

The Vazquez clan remains so true.

Through endless days, they forge their way,

Their name a light, come what may.

ABOUT THE CREATOR

Walter the Educator is one of the pseudonyms for Walter Anderson. Formally educated in Chemistry, Business, and Education, he is an educator, an author, a diverse entrepreneur, and he is the son of a disabled war veteran. "Walter the Educator" shares his time between educating and creating. He holds interests and owns several creative projects that entertain, enlighten, enhance, and educate, hoping to inspire and motivate you. Follow, find new works, and stay up to date with Walter the Educator™

at WaltertheEducator.com